ROAR

Betty Shamieh

BROADWAY PLAY PUBLISHING INC
224 E 62nd St, NY, NY 10065
www.broadwayplaypub.com
info@broadwayplaypub.com

ROAR

© Copyright 2004 by Betty Shamieh

All rights reserved. This work is fully protected under the copyright laws of the United States of America. No part of this publication may be photocopied, reproduced, stored in a retrieval system, or transmitted, in any form or by any means, electronic, mechanical, recording, or otherwise, without the prior permission of the publisher. Additional copies of this play are available from the publisher.

Written permission is required for live performance of any sort. This includes readings, cuttings, scenes, and excerpts. For amateur and stock performances, please contact Broadway Play Publishing Inc. For all other rights contact Ron Gwiazda, Abrams Artists Agency, 275 7th Ave, 26th fl, NY NY 10001, 646 486-4600.

First printing: Jan 2005; this printing: Oct 2011
I S B N: 978-0-88145-255-6

Book design: Marie Donovan
Word processing: Microsoft Word
Typographic controls: Xerox Ventura Publisher 2.0 P E
Typeface: Palatino
Printed and bound in the U S A

ROAR was first produced by The New Group (Scott Elliot, Artistic Director; Geoffrey Rich, Executive Director) opening on 7 April 2004. The cast and creative contributors were:

KARMEA . . . . Sarita Choudhury
IRENE . . . . Sherri Eldin
AHMED . . . . Joseph Kamal
HALA . . . . Annabella Sciorra
ABE . . . . Daniel Oreskes

Director . . . . Marion McClinton
Sets . . . . Beowulf Boritt
Costumes . . . . Mattie Ullrich
Lights . . . . Jason Lyons
Sound . . . . Ken Travis
Dramaturg . . . . Ian Morgan

CHARACTERS & SETTING

KAREMA, *a Palestinian-American woman, late thirties*
AHMED, *a Palestinian-American man, early forties*
IRENE, *a Palestinian-American teenage girl*
HALA, *a Palestinian woman, mid thirties*
ABE, *a Palestinian-American man, early fifties*

Place: Detroit, Michigan

Time: 1991

to Joseph Shamieh

ACT ONE

Scene One

(The setting: A living room in Detroit. This is the home of the Yacoub family. The living room and the doors of the kitchen, bathroom, and two bedrooms are visible. The bedroom doors are on opposite sides of the stage. The home has been converted out of the space above a small, but lucrative party store that they own. A party store is a liquor store that also sells some food items and there is one on practically every corner of downtown Detroit.)

(Outside, there is a neon sign "Ahmed's Liquor and Snacks" with a neon arrow pointing downward.)

(In the living room, there is an odd mix of European furniture covered in plastic and Middle Eastern embroidered tapestries.)

*(*KAREMA *sits at a table, methodically counting large stacks of money. There is plate heaping with peeled and sliced fruit on the table. She stops counting when first* IRENE*, then* AHMED *enter through the front door.)*

IRENE: Mom, I can sing! You should have heard me tonight. I have a voice that angels envy. I was hotter than hot.

KAREMA: People who are that great don't have to brag about it.

(Pause. IRENE *locks eyes with her mother who returns her stare innocently.)*

IRENE: You know, Mom...sometimes...forget it. *(Heads towards her room)*

KAREMA: You must be hungry. Have some fruit. *(Blocks* IRENE*'s way, and offers her the plate of fruit)*

IRENE: No.

AHMED: I'll take some.

*(*AHMED *takes the plate from* KAREMA *and sits down to eat.)*

IRENE: For your information, I wasn't bragging, Mom. I was just trying to tell you about something important that happened tonight. That was a mistake. *(Tries to step past* KAREMA*)*

KAREMA: *(Blocking her way)* Tell me.

AHMED: Tell her, Irene. You know, Karema, these figs are dry. *(Continues to chew with a sour expression on his face)*

KAREMA: I knew they weren't ripe. If that grocer doesn't give me back my money, I'll dump them on his—

*(*IRENE *tries to slip past her mother and head towards her room)*

KAREMA: Irene, don't go. I want to hear about your concert.

IRENE: It was an open-mike night. How many times have I explained to you that I perform at—

KAREMA:	IRENE: *(At the same time)*
You know what I mean.	—open mike nights and—

IRENE: —that I don't have concerts?

AHMED: Yet.

IRENE: Yet. Right, Dad. Thank God someone supports me around here.

KAREMA: You know I love to hear you sing.

AHMED: *(While chewing)* A producer [seemed to be]—

IRENE: Don't tell her. Nothing happened, Mom. Nothing at all.

KAREMA: Why are you angry at me?

IRENE: I'm not angry. You know why? Because not even you can make me angry tonight.

KAREMA: Good. You know what I always say. No one can make you angry unless you—

IRENE: *(Obviously furious now)* Not even you! *(She runs into her bedroom and slams the door.)*

KAREMA: *(Calling after her)* —let them.

(Music blares from IRENE*'s room.)*

AHMED: She wasn't that great.

*(*KAREMA *taps her ear—a "be quiet" gesture—and motions towards* IRENE*'s door.)*

AHMED: *(As loud as before)* But she wasn't bad either. I can make something out [of her]—

*(*KAREMA *grabs his arm.)*

KAREMA: *(Softly)* Be quieter.

AHMED: She can't hear us.

KAREMA: Yes, she can.

AHMED: What's the big deal?

KAREMA: I don't want you to hurt her feelings.

AHMED: You're the one who said she was bad. *(Picks up a fig)* Here's a ripe one. You take it.

KAREMA: No, you take it.

*(*AHMED *eats it.)*

KAREMA: All I said was that she should be more modest. What is it that she won't tell me, Ahmed?

AHMED: She did better than she normally does and a producer showed some interest in her. You should have come. You told Irene you would.

KAREMA: I told her I might. But you know that, if you go, I can't very well leave the store.

AHMED: We have workers—

KAREMA: If I let you run things, we'd be in the poorhouse.

AHMED: The poorhouse would be an improvement on this dump.

KAREMA: I know exactly why you want to live in those apartments of ours.

AHMED: Karema, I'm not going to explain myself about that anymore. I went by to check on that tenant's pipes.

KAREMA: *(Stops counting to face him)* She didn't even like you, Ahmed. That fat assed fake blond didn't even like you.

AHMED: I didn't like her either.

KAREMA: Well, that's not what she thought. *(Mimics an outraged but whiny Mid-Western voice)* Tell your husband not to drop by anymore. Tell him—

AHMED:	KAREMA: *(At the same time)*
American women think all Arab men are dirty.	I have a boyfriend and he's big...

KAREMA: And the way you behave certainly dispels that stereotype.

AHMED: I checked on all the other tenants' pipes too. Call up and ask them. *(Picks up phone and tries to hand it to her.)* Call up all our tenants right now and ask them.

(KAREMA *takes the phone from him and puts it down.)*

KAREMA: It is after midnight. *(She sits down and starts to count the money angrily but methodically.)*

AHMED: *(Hovering over her)* Why are you so suspicious of me?

KAREMA: Because I keep finding things like this in your pants pocket. *(Picks up a piece of paper under a stack of money and waves it in his face)*

AHMED: Why were you [going through my]—

KAREMA: I was doing the laundry.

*(*KAREMA *picks up program and rips it in half.*
AHMED *shakes his head wearily.)*

KAREMA: Why does it say that she's Egyptian?
What if someone we know [sees]—

AHMED: No one we know shows up at open mike nights.

IRENE: *(Off-stage)* Mom, it's none of your business.

KAREMA: *(Walking over to* IRENE*'s bedroom door)*
Oh, so your life is none of my business now, is it?

*(*KAREMA *opens the door of* IRENE*'s room.* IRENE *appears in the doorway, blocking her mother from entering.)*

IRENE: Don't come into my room.

KAREMA: I don't want to come into your room. If you want to be a part of this conversation, come out here.
I will not have you sit in your room and yell.

*(*IRENE*'s response is to slam the door in her mother's face. DKAREMA tries to open* IRENE*'s door. It is locked.)*

AHMED: Karema, Irene sings the blues and that's
an African-American thing. Egypt is part of Africa,
Palestine is technically—

AHMED:	KAREMA: *(At the same time)*
Part of Asia.	I know where I'm from.

AHMED: You look more legitimate...it is more strategic to package one's self that way.

KAREMA: The only problem is she's not.

AHMED: A blues singer with roots in the continent of Africa is an easy package to sell. Come on, Karema. Who in America has ever heard of a Palestinian blues singer?

KAREMA: Who in America has ever heard of a Palestinian anything?

AHMED: Why should Irene suffer on account of politics she knows nothing about? I'm right about this and you know it. Don't you see? Abe might now be willing to help Irene's career along—

KAREMA: Don't speak your brother's name in this house.

AHMED: Fine. I'm glad I did what I did, and you will be too. I only want what's best for Irene. *(Gently pulls her towards him)* Trust me, Karema.

KAREMA: *(Resists his embrace, but relents and allows herself to relax in his arms)* Why didn't you discuss this with me first?

AHMED: There's nothing to discuss. Something good might actually happen with this producer we met tonight, Karema. He said he remembered Irene from Star Search. His name is Dan Goldman.

(Pause. KAREMA *makes a motion to speak, but* AHMED *interjects.)*

AHMED: Goldman said he'd call soon and, when he does, you let him talk to me.

(The phone rings. IRENE *reenters and runs towards the phone.* KAREMA *and* AHMED *both reach for it, but* KAREMA *grabs it first.)*

KAREMA: Hello. *(She speaks in Arabic into the phone.)*

IRENE: What is she saying? What's happening?

AHMED: Your aunt is coming.

Scene Two

*(*HALA, KAREMA, *and* IRENE *enter.* IRENE *carries* HALA*'s luggage.)*

HALA: Oh, by the way, an American man asked me to marry him on the plane.

IRENE: What did you say?

HALA: No, of course. But it's nice to know that American men appreciate my charms as much as Arabs.

KAREMA: The appeal of a loose woman is universal, Hala. I could have told you that.

HALA: You should have. You would have saved me the long trip over here I had to take to find out.

KAREMA: You act as if you have somewhere else to go, Hala.

IRENE: Mom!

HALA: Don't worry, your mother and I like to tease one another. She doesn't really mean to imply that I am a loose woman. Not that loose women have it any worse than tight ones, right, Irene?

IRENE: You're funny, Aunty. And you're even prettier in real life than you are in the pictures. The one time my dad took me to meet my uncle Abe—

KAREMA: He's dead to us.

HALA: Is that crazy man still passing himself off as a Morrocan Jew? After all these years—

IRENE: An Egyptian Jew, actually.

KAREMA: I don't want his name mentioned in my house!

IRENE: As I was saying, my dad wants me to pretend to be Egyptian in case it might make it easier for my uncle to help me in my career. Uncle Abe told me that I look a little like you. Is it true that a super rich prince fell in love with you and you moved to Kuwait to be with him?

HALA:	KAREMA: *(At the same time)*
Maybe.	Hardly.

KAREMA: He was no prince.

(A police siren blares outside so KAREMA *has to speak up)*

KAREMA: That's for sure.

*(*KAREMA *gets up and gathers a few bags of parsley. The sound of the siren fades away.)*

IRENE: Tell me about him.

HALA: There's nothing to tell. *Habibtey,* I actually moved to Kuwait to be a music teacher. A quiet, unassuming music teacher. That's me. When is Ahmed coming up?

KAREMA: In another hour. Sorry he was so short with you. When it gets busy like that—

HALA: He wasn't short with me.

IRENE: I'm sure you had a lot of *(Pause),* you know, wild times in Kuwait, Aunty. Tell me everything.

KAREMA: If we're staying up, make yourselves useful.

*(*KAREMA *empties a huge pile of parsley on the coffee table in front of them and starts picking the leaves off their stems, arranging them in piles.* IRENE *also does so.)*

KAREMA: Well, join in, Hala. Do you need an invitation?

HALA: I'm tired from the flight.

KAREMA: Well, you're going to be hungry too, if I don't have this done today. Unless, of course, you—Hala—plan on taking care of dinner tomorrow by yourself while I'm at the store?

*(*HALA *picks up a stem and starts lazily picking off the leaves at a much slower rate than* IRENE *or* KAREMA.*)*

KAREMA: I didn't think so.

IRENE: So how come you never married, Aunty?

HALA: Because I could not be held responsible for the consequences. If I chose one man over another—world wars, destruction, mayhem would ensue. I love my fellow men too much to be the cause of all that suffering.

KAREMA: We know about how you love your fellow men.

IRENE: It's so getting old, Mom. I would not want to get with a Kuwaiti guy. They're darker than we are. Weird-looking, too. Why do they wear those dresses and scarf thing-ys on their heads?

KAREMA: Because they're proud—

HALA: Because they're ignorant.

KAREMA: They are proud of their—

HALA:	KAREMA: *(At the same time)*
Ignorance.	Heritage.

KAREMA: Well, anyway, you shouldn't judge a man by how he's dressed.

HALA: Judge him by how quickly he is ready to get undressed and, when you use that as your standard, you'll find that men are the same no matter where you go. Unless you can make men fall in love with you the way they fall in love with me.

KAREMA: But they couldn't have loved you that much, Hala. If they did, they would have let you stay, don't you think? Your ass was kicked out.

HALA: I wasn't kicked out. I've never been kicked out of anywhere in my life.

KAREMA: Did you suddenly stop being Palestinian? Even Ted Koppel said every Palestinian in Kuwait had to—

HALA: I don't want to talk about politics right now. I just got here, having recently survived the traumas of war. If you bring this up now, I might start having flashbacks.

KAREMA: When Iraq first invaded Kuwait, I think it was a mistake on [our part to]—

HALA: You don't change! I said shut up.

KAREMA:	HALA: *(At the same time)*
Don't ever talk to me that way.	I've had a rough day.

KAREMA: It's going to get rougher if you don't apologize. Remember you're in my house.

HALA: Okay, okay. I'm sorry. *(To* IRENE*)* You know why people like your mother get obsessed with politics, Irene? Because it's easier to get yourself all worked up about stuff you can't change than to deal with the things in your own life that you actually can.

IRENE: But, whose side were you on, Aunty? The Kuwaitis or the Iraqis?

HALA: Where did you get this kid from, Karema?

*(*KAREMA *shrugs.)*

HALA: Irene, where your mother and I come from, you are born into one side or the other. The only choice you make is whether or not to keep breathing.

KAREMA: That's a bit of an exaggeration—

HALA: Not for those who play by the rules. But, then, there are those who are naughty, naughty, naughty little Christian girls like your mother who run off and marry a Muslim—

IRENE: It must have caused the hugest scandal when my mom and dad hooked up.

KAREMA: Irene, there is something you need to know about your aunt. She has a problem with the truth. She never tells it.

HALA: If you are so honest, how could you deceive our poor sweet parents like that, Karema? *(Pause)* But, we won't go into all that. I'm sure your mother has told you the details plenty of times.

IRENE: My mom won't discuss it with me.

KAREMA: *(Picking up a piece of parsley)* Hala, look at this! You left half the stem on!

HALA: Relax.

IRENE: She always changes the subject.

HALA: I wonder why. The kid wants to hear the story, Karema, and I'm going to tell it. Either now or later. We are sharing a room, aren't we, Irene?

(IRENE *nods.)*

HALA: *Habibtey*, you are wrong about one thing. There was no scandal when your parents got married. Scandal is climbing on a top of a table at a wedding and shaking your breasts in the face of the groom.

KAREMA: Things you were famous for.

HALA: Among others. It's true. When I go to weddings, I can't see a bride next to her groom without thinking to myself "If I cornered your husband in a bathroom tonight, I wonder how long it would be before he broke his newly sworn vows."

KAREMA: And most people just go to weddings to be happy for the couple.

HALA: Most people are idiots.

IRENE: I'm sure she wasn't the first Christian girl to marry a Muslim guy.

HALA: Perhaps not. But it was a very bold thing to do. Even revolutionary. Wasn't it, my sweet sister?

KAREMA: I was young.

HALA: Not that young. Certainly old enough to get the itch. In fact, I think she was about your age, Irene.

IRENE: I'm fifteen.

HALA: She was exactly your age. Right, Karema?

(Pause. KAREMA *continues to pick the grape leaves off their stems, ignoring them.)*

IRENE: You must have really loved Dad to do that, Mom.

HALA: Irene, I can't believe she didn't tell you how she would drag me to see your father's boring concerts, where she would sit, stuck to her seat, and I do mean stuck—

KAREMA: Hala!

HALA: Anyway, she liked your dad more than the nice Christian boy our parents picked out for her. What was his name again? We always called him the tallest man in the universe.

IRENE: Why didn't you like that guy, Mom?

KAREMA: Because he was shorter than I was.

IRENE: But didn't you say he was—

HALA: He wasn't an inch over five feet. You see, back home we call people by their opposites. So you can never take anything that's said for face value. That's what makes our homeland such a lovely, lovely place.

KAREMA: As usual, you miss the point, Hala. We never talk of the good qualities people possess to protect them from the evil eye. Disparage what you love and you can keep it. No one will know its value and take it away.

HALA: Anyway. Karema, you should be ashamed of yourself. I can't believe I've been in this house, working so long, and no one even offered me a drink.

IRENE: I'm sorry. I didn't know you were thirsty.

HALA: You actually expect me to tell you?! You want to make your aunt beg?! We are a desert people, Irene. We know a guest could be dying of thirst, expiring in your living room because they're too embarrassed to ask for a drink.

IRENE: But we just came from the restaurant.

HALA: It doesn't matter! You look like an Arab. You've got to live like one. So, I expect that you'll follow our ancient custom of letting anyone into your home and not asking your guest to do anything—not even to tell you where they came from or who they are—for three whole days. Now get me a cup of tea.

(IRENE *exits.)*

KAREMA: Are the rumours true? *(Pause)* Tell me.

HALA: Karema, you know I get three days in which you can ask me no questions.

KAREMA: You're going to get one foot which you cannot dislodge from your asshole if you don't start talking. Our ancient custom! Please! Don't confuse the girl. The Bedouins don't even follow those rules anymore. Now, are the rumours true? We heard the Kuwaiti men threw all the Palestinian women out into the streets where—

HALA: No, of course not. It was a really boring takeover. At first, I thought there was going to be some action! You know I've always had a thing for Iraqi men. Now, Jordanians are another story. *(Pause.)* You should have seen the one at the American embassy I had to fuck to get to get a visa to come here.

KAREMA: So, that's how you got one?

HALA: How else? Jesus, he must have been four hundred pounds. I told myself "Hala, just imagine you're making love to two thin gorgeous men who are overwhelming you with their love and this won't feel so bad. Imagine that and you will enjoy this."

KAREMA: Did you?

HALA: No, but I didn't care. I had to get out.

KAREMA: I couldn't stay there either.

HALA: You'd stay. You wouldn't fuck anyone to get out of anything. Of course, I didn't have to leave Kuwait. But, I was not staying there after they kicked out the rest of the Palestinians. No way. Not me.

KAREMA: Liar.

HALA: Okay. Muhammed dumped me. It was considered unpatriotic to have a Palestinian piece of ass so I had to go.

KAREMA: He never offered to marry you?

HALA: Begged me at first. Unlike some people, I remember that my family can trace our Christian roots back to the time of Christ and that my ancestor was probably Mary Magdalene herself. So, I don't marry Muslims.

KAREMA: But you're a kept woman for them.

HALA: Many women share one husband with others and, even those that think they don't, really do. Now you tell me who is kept and who isn't. Irene!

(IRENE *reenters.)*

IRENE: Yes, Aunty?

HALA: I like fresh mint in my tea. Do you happen to grow your own mint?

KAREMA: Yes, which I'm sure you saw on the stoop downstairs.

IRENE: You want me to run downstairs and grab you a few leaves?

HALA: If you wouldn't mind.

IRENE: Of course not. *(Heads towards the door)*

KAREMA: It's late. I'll get it.

IRENE: No, Mom. I'm already up.

KAREMA: I said, I'll get it.

IRENE: I'll be fine. Dad's downstairs. He can see the stoop from the cash register.

HALA: You act like you're afraid to let the kid outside.

KAREMA: There are drunks who hang around.

IRENE: Because they know we sell liquor after hours.

KAREMA: Put on your coat. I'll watch you from the window.

(IRENE *leaves out the front door without putting on her coat.* KAREMA *stands by the window and looks out of it.)*

HALA: So, the kid really knows nothing about our life?

KAREMA: No.

HALA: And you want to keep it that way. Fine. Don't worry. I'll be gone sooner than you know it.

KAREMA: You're welcome here, Hala. You're welcome anywhere I am.

HALA: I'm not staying long. But, while I'm here, Karema, let's get one thing straight. I'm not going to talk about things I don't want to talk about. You don't really want to know what went on in Kuwait. You think you do, but you don't. Because talking—

KAREMA: HALA: *(At the same time)*
I didn't mean to upset you——never does a damn thing.

*(*KAREMA *and* HALA *stop speaking abruptly when* IRENE *enters with mint leaves in her hand.)*

HALA: You know your mother never changes, Irene.

IRENE: No, she doesn't. *(She exits into the kitchen.)*

HALA: I bet you still hide your money under your mattress.

KAREMA: Now I keep a gun next to it.

HALA: I'm not going to take your money. I've never stolen a thing in my life. Well, except for things that get up and follow me out on their own two legs.

*(*IRENE *reenters carrying a tray of nuts, various Middle Eastern dips, and sliced vegetables.)*

IRENE: I thought you might like a little something, Aunty.

HALA: Oh, that's so sweet of you to want to feed your aunt. But I've got to watch my figure. Soon, I'm going to pay an old friend a visit.

KAREMA: If you're talking about Abe—

HALA: I have a lot of old friends. Where's the tea, Irene?

IRENE: The water hasn't boiled. Do you want sugar in it?

HALA: Never. Remember that.

IRENE: Of course. After you have your tea, I would love to hear you sing.

HALA: You're like your mother. I ask for one cup of tea and you want to make me work for it.

IRENE: I've heard so much about the midnight concerts you gave in Jerusalem that even the Jews attended.

KAREMA: I've got an idea. While you're here, Hala, you can make yourself useful. You can teach Irene how to sing the *mow'alla'at.*

IRENE: What's that?

KAREMA: Traditional Arabic songs. For every day you spend here, Hala, you will spend one hour teaching Irene. Starting tomorrow. Understood?

HALA: Ask like a normal person. Say 'Hey, Sis. I need help. I need your help. Teach my daughter some music.' And I'd gladly do it.

IRENE: Nice of you both to decide upon on my life, but I'm way too busy to learn Arabic music.

*(*HALA *raises an eyebrow)*

IRENE: You see, this big music producer—

HALA: Well, that was quite a plane ride. It took so long to get here I thought I never would. Don't worry about the tea, Irene. I've got to get to bed. *(Gets up and walks towards the master bedroom)*

IRENE: You're going the wrong way, Aunty. That's my mom and dad's room. *(She points to her bedroom.)*

*(*HALA *changes direction and exits into* IRENE*'s room.)*

KAREMA: Irene, your aunt is—

IRENE: Is what?

KAREMA: Just don't believe everything she says. She lies a lot. For no reason. About silly things. Don't believe everything she says.

IRENE: I don't believe everything anyone says.

KAREMA: Good. Get to bed, Irene. I want you rested for school tomorrow. Good-night.

IRENE: Good-night.

(After IRENE *exits into her bedroom,* KAREMA *walks over to the door and attempts to eavesdrop as the lights fade.)*

Scene Three

*(*IRENE *knocks on her parents' bedroom door.)*

IRENE: Get up! Mom's going to kill you.

*(*HALA *enters from* IRENE*'s room.)*

AHMED: *(Offstage)* Leave me alone, Irene.

IRENE: Get downstairs and help Mom with the morning rush.

HALA: Can't a person get some sleep around here?

IRENE: Sorry. *(Bangs on the door again)* Dad, the tea's on the stove. Bye, Aunty. *(As she gathers her book-bag)* We have this thing called a whistling tea kettle. When the water gets hot, the whistle [will blow]—

HALA: We have whistling tea kettles in Kuwait.

IRENE: Sorry. I didn't know. It seems kind of Third World to me.

HALA: I had finer things than you can imagine in Kuwait. If you visited me, you would have been so jealous, it would have made you want to tear your eyes out.

(Pause)

IRENE: I guess it's a good thing I didn't visit then.

(She smiles, HALA *doesn't smile back.)*

HALA: Irene, your mother wants me to begin your Arabic music lessons today. What time will you [be home]—

IRENE: Nice of you to offer, but I can't. You see, this really important music producer is interested in my work and he's going to call any day now.

HALA: But, until he calls, why not—

IRENE: Until he calls, I've got to spend every minute preparing to rock his world, so he agrees to make a demo. Gotta go. I'm late for school.

*(*IRENE *kisses* HALA *and exits. Then* AHMED *enters from his bedroom, looking exhausted and messily dressed. He sees* HALA *lounging on the couch in her nightgown and stops in his tracks.)*

HALA: Good morning.

AHMED: *(Still standing in the same spot)* Good morning.

HALA: Did you sleep well?

AHMED: Yes, but too briefly. Karema likes to open the store at the crack of dawn so we can make money off the kids going to school.

HALA: Karema is...industrious.

AHMED: Insane is more like it. I should go help her.

HALA: Stay a moment, Ahmed. The water's on the stove. A man should at least have a cup of tea before he starts his day.

AHMED: You're right.

HALA: Of course I am. Um, Ahmed. I have a huge favor to ask.

AHMED: What?

HALA: Do you think that you could—at some point today—give me a ride? I have an old friend I need to visit.

AHMED: *(Awkwardly)* I'm sure if you ask Karema, she'll take you.

HALA: Yeah, of course. I just didn't want to bother her.

AHMED: Karema'd be happy to do it, I'm sure. While you're here, Hala, you got to drag her out of that store once in a while. All those hours she makes us put into it is starting to dull our brains. But, I shouldn't complain. Karema's got us where we are today.

(HALA looks around, non-plussed.)

HALA: She did, did she?

AHMED: You wouldn't know it by how we live, but we're doing really well. Karema saves every penny to buy property and property always goes up. I tell Karema, if we moved to Jordan, we could live like royalty just off the rent we get from our apartments alone. Hell, we could even live like royalty off that rent here if we wanted to.

HALA: Karema would never live in Jordan.

AHMED: I know. She hates it. All because of the, you know, little mistreatment of your family during Black September.

HALA: There was more than a little mistreatment.

AHMED: Still, that was a long time ago. *(Getting more comfortable and animated)* Times are better now. I would love to live there, but Karema likes it in America. She says here no one tries to pretend we belong. Is that why you left?

HALA: Kind of.

AHMED: I went back last year. Alone. It's been twenty years and everyone there still recognizes me from the concerts I gave in Amman. Can you believe it?

HALA: That doesn't surprise me at all. You were really something. I bet if you went back today and starting holding concerts, people would come out in droves.

AHMED: Do you really think so?

HALA: I do. You should think about trying it.

AHMED: It would be so nice to perform our music again. But, I can't leave Karema alone in the store that long.

HALA: That's a shame. Everyone loved your concerts.

AHMED: Yeah. Even Karema. Not anymore. Now, I go to the basement of some apartments we own to practice. Don't mention it to Karema but, whenever I go to fix some pipe or toilet, I give myself an hour or two to play. Karema thinks I'm the slowest handyman around. I go there because she won't let me play my *tubleh* in the house. She says she hates the sound of it. I don't understand. She used to come to every concert I held.

HALA: She never went for the music. She would go just to hear you say the little speech you made every time you finished playing. What was it that you used to say....

AHMED: *(Stands up)* "I hope this music caught your heart off guard and held it, so that your mind could wander to a place where you could love anyone, whether Muslim, Jew, or Christian, in this land that belongs to us all and that one day soon we will learn to share."

(Pause. HALA *bursts into laughter.)*

HALA: You were always such a good bullshitter.

AHMED: *(A little miffed)* You know the funny thing is, I used to believe it.

HALA: I'm sorry. Of course you did.

AHMED: Remember that time there was fighting near the border and the power went out?

HALA: Which time?

AHMED: The time we stayed and held our concert in the dark. I can't believe you don't remember! Abe and Karema wanted to go with the people that were going, and you wanted to stay with me and the others who wouldn't leave.

HALA: Oh, yeah, that night! Of course.

AHMED: No one could forget it. It was me who struck up the first notes of *Biktub Ismik*. Soon enough, it was clear none of us were leaving. That was my favorite concert actually—with the mics gone, the lights gone, each singer in one corner and what was left of the band wading through the crowd in the dark. I could hear your voice the loudest. I remember trying to time my beat to sound of your voice.

HALA: Really?

AHMED: Yeah. I would not have given up playing that concert if it cost my life, and it damn near might have. Then, the finale! When we put down our instruments and everyone, audience and performers, stood up and sang in the dark. *(Sings) Biktub ismuck ya habibi alla' hawr a-teek. (Translation: I carve your name in the wood of old trees/You write my name in the sand in the street/Tomorrow when it rains, yours will remain, but my name will be erased, obliterated, gone, forgotten)*

HALA & AHMED: *(Sings) Tiktub ismey ya habibi alla' rumlel tarik.*

*(*HALA *gets up and begins to bellydance and* AHMED *stands up and claps in time. They sing the next part louder and stronger—it's the chorus of the song.)*

HALA & AHMED: *Wa bookra lema itsheety, ismeeme biyimha'aa...*

*(*IRENE *enters from the front door to see* HALA *and* AHMED *dancing and singing.* HALA *goes over to* IRENE *and raises* IRENE*'s arms in the air, making* IRENE *sway with her.)*

HALA: Dance with me.

IRENE: *(Trying to pull her arms free)* I don't dance, Aunty.

HALA: *(Still maintaining her grasp on* IRENE*'s hands and keeping them in the air as she sways her hips)* Shake your hips. *(Singing) Ismeeme biyimha'aa.* (HALA *stops singing and lets* IRENE*'s arms go)* How are you going to catch a man if you can't dance?

*(*IRENE *shrugs.)*

AHMED: Why aren't you at school?

IRENE: *(Not realizing she is wearing her coat)* I, uh, came back because I forgot my coat.

AHMED: You are wearing your coat.

IRENE: Okay, Dad. Don't tell Mom, but I don't want to miss Goldman's call.

AHMED: Irene, we've got an answering machine. I can't believe you're cutting school again.

HALA: Oh, let her stay. It's my first day here.

AHMED: She's on academic probation.

IRENE: Come on, Dad. Don't rat on me to Mom. She'll guilt-trip me about how her family couldn't afford her [to keep her in school]—

AHMED: Irene, I'm not going to lie to Mom.

IRENE: You're supposed to be in the store, right? I won't tell her I saw you and you don't tell her that you saw me.

AHMED: All right, but go straight back to school, Irene.

IRENE: Thanks, Dad. Bye, Aunty. *(She exits.)*

AHMED: I don't know what I'm going to do with that kid. She's flunking out, she doesn't know how to make friends. I thought it was just awkward for her with Americans. So I started taking her to the mosque, though it bores me to tears so, you know, she has a community of some sort, but she doesn't talk to the kids there either.

HALA: She'll be fine. Worse comes to worse, you can marry her off.

AHMED: To whom? I've encouraged her to pursue music. I think I can make a singer out of her. But, she doesn't listen to me, she gets nervous on-stage.

HALA: You will make something out of her.

AHMED: Why do you say that?

HALA: Because she's your daughter. And I remember what kind of musician you were. You have brought her here, where she will have chances that you didn't.

AHMED: That's the only reason I came here. The only reason I let Karema convince me to stay.

HALA: She will succeed. I believe that with all my heart. You have nothing to worry about, Ahmed.

AHMED: Thanks, Hala. It's good to have you around. You remind me of the old times.

HALA: If your wife had her way, I'd already be gone.

AHMED: What do you mean?

HALA: I know how cheap your wife is. She begrudges me the food I eat.

AHMED: You're her sister. She's not that cheap.

HALA: Even if she isn't, I'd rather live on the streets than live off of her. I've got to see Abe. You know Karema won't take me. Can you drive me to see him?

AHMED: Have you been in touch with him since—

HALA: Since I left him waiting at the airport? No.

AHMED: I'm not sure that it's a good idea....

HALA: What? Do you actually think he still hates me?

AHMED: Can you blame him?

HALA: Of course. You can always blame someone, whether or not they deserve it is another question entirely. He loved me.

AHMED: But you broke his heart.

HALA: So, I know exactly what part needs fixing. I hurt his pride, so I'll give up mine. I'll beg for him. Don't tell him I'm here, don't tell him a thing, just take me to him. Please, Ahmed. Right now!

AHMED: I would, but Karema won't let me off work and you know how she feels about him...I know! At noon today I'm supposed to go to the apartment building to fix a toilet. I'll tell Karema I'm taking care of that and we can go to his office.

HALA: Thank you, Ahmed. Oh, my God! What am I going to wear? Look at me, Ahmed. Do I look older to you?

AHMED: You look amazing. Abe will take you back. I know it.

HALA: You think so?

AHMED: I know so.

HALA: Really? How?

AHMED: I don't think any man could resist you.

(The tea kettle whistles loudly.)

AHMED: *(Speaking over the noise as he heads towards the kitchen)* Irene leaves the kettle on to make sure I get up. I'll be right back.

*(*AHMED *exits through the door to the kitchen. The whistle is silenced. While he is gone,* HALA *exits into* IRENE*'s room.* AHMED *returns with two tea cups. He looks around the room for a second, places a cup down on a table near* IRENE*'s door, and takes his cup with him out the front door.)*

Scene Four

*(*IRENE *enters. She hits the button the answering machine. It says "No new messages."* IRENE *frowns. She takes a business card out of her bag. She dials, but hangs up before speaking. Pause. She dials again.)*

IRENE: *(Speaking nervously, trying to sound sexy but her voice has a squeaky edge to it)* Hi. May I speak to Dan Goldman please? *(Pause)* Irene Yacoub. He gave me his card. *(Pause)* Yes, well, can you tell him when he gets off the other line that another company, Right On Records, is really interested in me and before I commit to them, I'd like to talk to Mr Goldman. You know, I think it's only fair since he did approach me first and all. Yes. *(Pause)* Um, uh, when do you think he'll call me back? Uh, just so I can give my answer to Abe and the folks at Right On Records? Do you know the folks at Right On? *(Pause)* Yes, most people have heard of them.

*(*HALA *enters from* IRENE*'s bedroom.* IRENE *brings her finger to her lips, making a "be quiet, I'm on the phone" gesture wildly and repeatedly.* HALA *smiles wryly and steps closer to* IRENE*, not hiding her attempt to listen)*

IRENE: If you ask around, I'm sure they'll tell you that it's an important company. But, you know, I do want to be fair to Dan, so I'm letting him know that he should call me. *(Pause)* Please do. And thank you. Yeah, my number is 242-1948. He probably has it, but just in case. Thank you.

HALA: What was that about?

IRENE: You have to promise not to tell my mom or dad, especially not my dad.

HALA: I promise.

IRENE: I just called this important producer. I think if he thinks that other producers are interested in me, he'll sign me.

HALA: Have you talked to Abe about this?

IRENE: No. Uncle Abe won't help me, I'm just saying that so that this producer gets a move on.

HALA: I understand, but don't you think this man is going to think it's a little strange when he figures out that you and Abe have the same last name?

IRENE: You're right. Oh, shit. That was really dumb.

HALA: *Habibtey*, if you're going to lie, I must teach you how to be better at it. Never mind. I'm sure that this producer will be so excited to sign you that he won't look into details like that. You know, this man you just called might be really impressed if he knew you knew Arabic music.

IRENE: I don't have time to think about that right now, Aunty. *(She heads towards her bedroom.)*

HALA: What if this man can't help you, Irene?

IRENE: He's a big-time producer. Of course he can help me. And he will. He was really interested in me, even my dad says so.

HALA: Becoming a singer is a hard thing to try to do.

IRENE: I'm not trying to do anything. I am a singer, Aunty.

HALA: I know, but—

IRENE: But I might not be any good? I might not make it? Is that what you were going to say?

HALA: I was going to say that I wish you luck, Irene. I hope you get further than I did, because I once wanted to be a singer and I wanted it as badly as you do. You know, I have a secret too.

IRENE: What?

HALA: I'm not going to be here much longer. Don't tell your mom, but I saw Abe earlier today. I think him and I are going to get back together.

IRENE: Really?

HALA: He said he needed some time to think, but it's going to work out. I'm going to make damn sure it does.

IRENE: Are you going to convert to Judaism too?

HALA: Don't be silly. Abe hasn't really converted. Like I said, we're taking it slow, but I think he's planning to get me my own apartment soon. At least, that's what I suggested.

IRENE: Really?

HALA: If that happens, I might help make the lie you told about Abe wanting to work with you come true. But in the meanwhile, your mom wants me to teach you about Arabic music. She says I can't stay here, she won't feed me, unless I teach you some songs, give you a foundation—

IRENE: She doesn't really mean that. She just likes to...

HALA: Make people miserable? Yes, that she does. But would you mind doing me a favor, can we just pretend I'm teaching you stuff? She'll never know till it's too late and I'm already gone. Sound like a deal?

IRENE: Okay.

HALA: Great. Less work for me. So how are things, Irene? Any boyfriends?

IRENE: *(Defensive)* No. I'm focused on music right now.

HALA: Well, if you have to give up men in order to be a singer, it's no wonder I didn't make it. *(Beat)* I know you plan to be a singer, you're always talking about it, but why?

IRENE: Why what?

HALA: Why do you want to be a singer? You obviously want it as much as I did. Why do you want it so bad?

IRENE: It's hard to explain.

HALA: When did you decide you wanted to be a singer?

IRENE: When I was very young.

HALA: How young?

IRENE: I don't remember. Six or seven.

HALA: Six or seven?

IRENE: I don't know. For as long as I can remember—

HALA: I'm interested in how the idea to be a singer first came into your head. Was it when you heard someone else sing? Were you knocked off your feet by the sound of another human voice?

IRENE: A homeless woman used to sing Billie Holliday for change on our corner. I'd rush home after school to sit in that window and listen—Mom didn't let me play outside. Her voice made me want to live on the streets.

In my mind, I connected being homeless with being able to sing like that.

HALA: Do you know a song about that experience?

IRENE: What experience? What are you talking about?

HALA: A song about the experience of hearing another sing, which moves you to try and sing yourself. Do you know a song like that?

IRENE: No.

HALA: I do. And I can to teach it to you.

(Pause)

IRENE: Well, if it's a song about singing, then I guess I wouldn't mind learning it. I thought you wanted to teach me some political mumbo-jumbo songs.

HALA: No. You're going to have to prove yourself worthy, you're going to have to beg me to teach you political mumbo-jumbo songs. The song about singing is called *Junnelee wa Kudoo Aynaya.*

IRENE: You have to translate it.

HALA: I will. The title literally means sing a note and take my eyes in exchange. *(Sings) Junnelee wa Kudoo Aynaya*. Now you try, Irene.

IRENE: Take my eyes in exchange? How stupid.

HALA: There are very few things I respect in this world, Irene. Arabic music is one of them. So please—

IRENE: Arabic sounds so ugly. I never speak it in public. It sounds like spitting. *(She makes spitting sounds.)* I'm going to take your eyeballs and spit on you.

HALA: I feel like slapping you across your face.

IRENE: What?

HALA: As I was saying, what the title really means is take what is integral, necessary to my existence, in exchange. Sing me one note and take my eyes, I will not need them. When I want to see, I know you'll let me look through yours. That is how you have to be struck by music in order to want to create it. Do you agree?

IRENE: Yes.

HALA: Then the singer, who starts out as the listener begging to exchange her eyes for a few more notes, begins to sing herself. These are the words she sings:

She says I'm going to sing and sing and sing."

IRENE: *(Non-plussed)* Sing and sing and sing? Okay.

HALA: But the connotation is...when you translate it, it's more like *(Pauses for a moment and speaks haltingly as she chooses her words carefully)* I'm going to hum and sing and roar *(To herself)* That's it. I'm going to hum and sing and roar, make my listeners drunk on sound. Now, in Arabic—

IRENE: Just teach me the translation, Aunty. I want to sing it in English.

HALA: God forbid. You can't sing this in English.

IRENE: Why not? I'll even dedicate it you, Aunty. You're coming to my open mike later tonight, right?

HALA: Not if you plan on butchering the *mow'alla'at.* I will not let you sing this song in English. It will sound like shit in English.

IRENE: It won't sound like shit.

HALA: It will in comparison. In Arabic, it sounds like perfection, like a combination of words that existed before humans were here to make up words. Learn it in Arabic or don't learn it at all. But I'm telling you, Irene, if you learn to sing this song, then you can sing just about anything.

IRENE: Well, then, let me learn it.

(HALA picks up the 'oud *[Middle Easter guitar] and plays the tune.)*

HALA: We can try. But I don't know if I really *can* teach you. I mean, Arabic music isn't so easy to learn.

IRENE: I can handle it, Aunty.

HALA: I guess we'll see. *(Stops and starts the tune from the beginning)* You know a song is good when you hear the first note, and it makes you want to stick around to listen to the last. This is the intro.

IRENE: That sounds cool. Like a guitar.

HALA: *(Stops playing abruptly and hugs the* 'oud *close to her chest)* A guitar? Do not insult my *'oud.*

IRENE: Okay, okay.

(HALA resumes playing)

IRENE: Let me try.

HALA: One thing at a time, kid. You can do anything you want as long as you remember to tackle one thing at a time.

(AHMED and KAREMA enter and sit down to listen. HALA continues playing.)

KAREMA: I love this song. *(Begins to sing) Juneelee sh-waya, sh-waya.*

(The phone rings. Everyone rushes for it.)

IRENE: I've got it! I've got it!

(KAREMA answers the phone.)

KAREMA: Hello? *(Pause)* Oh, hello, Mrs Rivington. *(Her tone is suddenly obsequious.)* How is your cat? *(Pause)* Yes, he is. *(She glances at AHMED.)* Of course, I'll get him right away, Mrs Rivington.

(KAREMA *hands* AHMED *the phone.)*

IRENE: Come on, Aunty. Let's work in my room.

*(*HALA *plays as she walks to* IRENE*'s room.* IRENE *follows her. Off-stage is the sound of* HALA *playing the* 'oud.*)*

AHMED: Hi, Mrs Rivington. *(Pause)* I know. I'm sorry, but we had a major problem in another apartment I had to take care of. *(Pause)* I understand. *(Pause)* I understand. All I can say is I'm sorry. *(Pause)* No, please don't complain to the owner. Please. It will never happen again. Tomorrow I'll fix it and do anything else you need done in the apartment. What time is best for you? *(Pause)* Tomorrow at ten, it is. *(Pause)* No, I won't be late. Bye, now.

KAREMA: Why didn't you fix the lady's toilet?

AHMED: I have to get ready for Irene's open-mike night.

KAREMA: I'm asking you a question.

AHMED: By the time I changed the hinges on the laundry door, I had to get back to help you with the after-school rush.

KAREMA: Why did you tell me you had fixed it?

AHMED: I didn't want to deal with you saying I work too slow. We should just hire a plumber anyway. I can't do everything around here!

KAREMA: Lower your voice. You hardly do everything.

AHMED: Let's put it this way. I do everything you want me to do. You tell me when to get up, work, breathe, and shit—and I do it. But I'm sick of you putting me in a position where I have to kiss the ass of some old white bitch—

KAREMA: What would we do if Mrs Rivington wanted to follow up and complain to the owner?!

AHMED: It would be your fault for making me pretend to be the super in the first place. Why you're so sure people wouldn't rent the apartments if they think Arabs own them, I'll never know! *(Exits into the bathroom and slams the door)*

(Pause. IRENE *opens the door of her bedroom and sticks her head out to see what's going on.)*

KAREMA: Keep playing.

Scene Five

*(*AHMED *is on stage, adjusting a very stylish hat on his head.* KAREMA *enters through the front door.)*

KAREMA: Look at you. Dressed up like a teenager. Are you so eager to see your brother?

AHMED: Abe said he might even be able to get us backstage passes to meet Prince.

KAREMA: Since when did he start giving us backstage passes? He's only doing it so he can see Hala.

AHMED: Can you blame him? I mean, since he loved her all those years. Besides, we've got to be nice to Abe. That guy Goldman hasn't called yet. Abe said he would think about getting Irene's career started.

KAREMA: What's there to think about? Abe owns the damn record company. If he wants to help her, he can. How did Irene do at her concert?

*(*IRENE *enters from the front door in time to hear the word "concert".)*

IRENE: Open-mike night.

AHMED: Hi, Irene.

IRENE: *(Ignoring her father's greeting)* Hi, Mom.

AHMED: Irene, stop this silliness now.

KAREMA: What's the problem here?

IRENE: No problem. I'm just not speaking to Dad ever again.

KAREMA: What happened?

IRENE: What happened is my father and your sister were supposed to hear me sing last night. Instead, they somehow managed to disappear when it was time for my slot.

AHMED: We didn't know they were going to switch the line-up. We had to go outside because Hala was coughing up a storm from the smoke.

KAREMA: You left Irene alone in a nightclub?

AHMED: It was just for a minute. I didn't want her coughing to disturb your performance.

IRENE: Tell the truth, Dad. The bartender told me you went upstairs to jam with the regulars and that's why you left.

AHMED: Okay, I played a song or two.

KAREMA: Are you crazy?

AHMED: I haven't had a chance to perform in years. She was with the other singers.

IRENE: I don't know them! When you didn't come back, I got nervous. I did awful.

KAREMA: I can't believe you, Ahmed.

IRENE: Mr Goldman could have been in the audience.

AHMED: I checked. He wasn't.

IRENE: I know, but he could have been! You know what, Dad? *(Pulls out Goldman's card and places it in from of her dad)* I called Goldman yesterday and, when he signs me, I'm going to pretend I don't know you.

AHMED: You called Goldman?

IRENE: Yes.

AHMED: What did he say?

IRENE: I spoke to his assistant. I hinted that another music producer was interested in signing me.

AHMED: That's not true.

IRENE: I know that. *(Pause)* I hinted that the music producer was Uncle Abe.

KAREMA: Maybe it's a good thing that she called, Ahmed. She won't have to wait by the phone [anymore]—

AHMED: Karema, stay out of this. Irene, what is this "I hinted" shit? Either you said that or you didn't.

KAREMA: Ahmed, watch your language.

AHMED: I said, stay out of this.

IRENE: Don't worry. I didn't say he was my uncle, Dad.

AHMED: Goddamn it, Irene, you are one stupid little— *(Begins to complete his sentence with the word "bitch")*

KAREMA: *(Cutting him off)* Ahmed!

AHMED: It's our fault as much as yours that you're spoiled, Irene, but the world out there isn't going to let you get away with things like we do.

IRENE: I'm so spoiled. If people could see how great I've got it here, I'd be the envy of every girl in America.

AHMED: You are spoiled. Look at you. Do you ever even offer to help out in the store after school? Huh? Answer me. I said, answer me.

KAREMA: Ahmed, stop it.

IRENE: You never ask me to.

KAREMA: That's right, Ahmed. We never ask her to. We want her to have time for school.

AHMED: And still you barely manage to pass your classes.

IRENE: I'm focused on music.

AHMED: Your mother and I slave all day and half the night, so you can wear designer clothes and take private music lessons and bitch at me because I'm not doing everything you want all the time.

IRENE: You left me alone!

AHMED: You've been singing on-stage since you were six. You should be able to handle doing one goddamn open-mike night alone. I give up! I'll be honest, it's hard to get people interested in you, but I do my best. And you go and fuck it up! Now you've gotten Abe involved and [he's going to be mad at me]—

(HALA *enters, wearing very sexy clothing.)*

AHMED: Hi, Hala.

HALA: Well, are we going or not?

AHMED: Yeah. Sorry to make you wait.

IRENE: God forbid her highness has to wait.

HALA: I already apologized for not hearing you sing. One mistake, one apology. That's how it goes, kid.

IRENE: Whatever, Aunty. Why don't you come with us to the concert, Mama?

(HALA *puts on her coat and puts lipstick on.)*

KAREMA: I won't take anything from that man.

IRENE: You can't leave me alone with these two retards.

(HALA *raises an eyebrow, but continues primping.)*

AHMED: Talk to me like that again, Irene, and I'll slap you.

KAREMA: Watch yourself, Ahmed. Watch yourself.

AHMED: Tell your daughter to watch herself, Karema. She needs to learn some respect. In fact, for calling Goldman when I told you not to, Irene, you're going to be punished. You're staying home tonight.

IRENE: What?!

HALA: Ahmed, whatever Irene did, it can't be that bad. Irene goes or I don't go. And, Karema, you should come with us to the concert.

AHMED: She can't. She has to mind the store.

HALA: Fuck the store just this once, Karema.

KAREMA: Money from the store has been feeding your face for the past week. It's not always a good idea to fuck what feeds you.

HALA: It's a strategy that's worked pretty well for me, Sis.

KAREMA: Then why are you living off of us?

AHMED: We've got to go. She has to stay or I have to stay to mind the store. Everyone who wants to go, get in the car.

IRENE: Are you sure you can't come, Mom?

KAREMA: Yes, *habibtey*. Have fun with the prince.

(IRENE, AHMED, *and* HALA *exit.* KAREMA *begins to straighten up the room and notices Goldman's card. She picks it up and looks at it. Then, she goes to the phone and dials.)*

KAREMA: Hello. Is Mr Goldman there? *(Pause)* Okay, but can you please tell him that Karema Yacoub, Irene's mother, needs to talk to him. Can I ask you a question?

You're the person my daughter spoke to earlier, right? *(Pause)* Irene Yacoub, that's right. Mr Goldman has not called my daughter back. I know what that means. There is a saying in Arabic—no answer is an answer.

*(A siren blares outside—*KAREMA *has to speak up. The siren fades.)*

KAREMA: I'm calling because I want to see if he would be more interested in working with her if I paid for everything it cost for him to help her. *(Pause)* But things can work that way if he wants them to. *(Pause)* No, I'm not joking. I'm not poor. How much can it cost to produce a record? *(Her jaw drops)* I-I-I. Six hundred thousand! That's outrageous. No, don't hang up! I'll pay you. I'll sell my apartments and I'll pay you, but only three hundred thousand and not a penny more! *(Pause)* Hello? *(She dials.)* Hello. I think we got cut off. *(Pause)* I understand. You seem like a nice girl. Can you do me a favor? I have to tell my daughter your boss doesn't want to work with her. You tell people that all the time, so I was wondering if you could tell me—if you know—how to tell my daughter in a way that won't hurt her?

Scene Six

(It is morning. IRENE *enters from her room and rushes around, gathering her things. There is a knock at the door. Irene opens it.* HALA *is wearing the clothes she wore last night and she looks like she slept in them.)*

IRENE: Look what the cat dragged in.

HALA: *(Angry)* What?!

IRENE: Hi. Thanks so much for telling my dad to let me come last night. He got madder than I thought he would [because I]—

HALA: Irene, aren't you late for school?

IRENE: No. Did Uncle Abe take you to an after-party? I heard there was [a big one]—

HALA: No.

IRENE: Are you okay, Aunty?

HALA: Run along, kid.

IRENE: Okay. *(She gathers her things, but leaves her coat and exits.)*

(The tea kettle whistles sharply off-stage. HALA *jumps.)*

HALA: Why don't they use a fucking alarm clock in this house?

*(*AHMED *enters, glances at* HALA, *and darts into the kitchen. The sound of the kettle is silenced.* AHMED *returns with a cup of tea.)*

AHMED: *(Handing her the tea)* Are you okay?

HALA: *(Taking it)* Your brother could learn a few lessons from you on how to be a gentleman.

AHMED: What did he say, Hala?

HALA: He told me I deserved to end up how I am—broke and alone. I said that I did. You see, when people try to insult you and you agree with them, it usually takes the wind out of their sails. So, when he said I was a lazy little whore who would go with any man who had two pennies to rub together—

AHMED: No!

HALA: —I said that I was. Then, he said he didn't have two pennies to rub together—that he'd be willing to give me, at any rate.

AHMED: He shouldn't talk to you like that!

HALA: He wouldn't even drive me back here. Or give me cab fare.

AHMED: What about the hundred dollars I gave you?

HALA: I wanted to give it back to you. If I didn't have it, I wouldn't have been able to get back here this morning. I don't have much of it left. *(Takes out a few dollars from her purse and offers it to him)* Here, take it.

AHMED: Where did you spend that much...don't worry about it. Keep it. *(Gently closes her hand around the bills and leaves his hand cupped around hers)*

HALA: *(Slides her hand out from under his hand after a beat and puts the bills back in her purse)* I wanted to have a home with him. And children! Never wanted things like that before. Then, I did. All at once, so sharply, like a person born blind who figures out that everyone else can see. But he said he never really loved me in the first place—

AHMED: He's stupid.

HALA: He told me about the coin toss.

AHMED: The coin toss?! He and I promised we'd never tell either of you. Karema's been right about him all along. He's a son of a bitch. He'd be lucky to have you. Any man would be lucky to have you.

HALA: Yeah, sure. One thing about me, Ahmed,
is I always knew I'd know when I was washed up.
I'm just a shadow of what I was—

AHMED: No! You're not.

HALA: Even that is just a shadow of what I should have been.

AHMED: You're beautiful and nice and can sing like an—

(HALA kisses him. AHMED pulls away.)

HALA: I'm sorry.

*(*AHMED *kisses her. As the kiss gets more passionate, the door pops open.* IRENE *sees their embrace.)*

IRENE: *(As she exits quickly)* Hi.

*(*AHMED *and* HALA *jump away from one another and see the open door.* IRENE *is already gone—making it unclear to them what she saw.)*

AHMED: Oh, my God!

HALA: She didn't see anything.

(Pause)

AHMED: I've got to go to work.

*(*AHMED *exits out the front door.* HALA *is alone on-stage. Lights out)*

END OF ACT ONE

ACT TWO

Scene Seven

*(*IRENE *sits alone writing in the dark.* AHMED *tiptoes out of his room and heads towards* IRENE*'s room.)*

IRENE: Hi, Dad.

AHMED: Irene, you scared me. What are you doing up?

IRENE: Making music.

AHMED: You can't sing. It's the middle of the night.

IRENE: *(Continues to mark up the sheet she is working on and avoiding his gaze)* I'm composing.

*(*HALA *enters from* IRENE*'s bedroom.)*

HALA: Can't a person get to sleep around here?

AHMED: Sorry, Hala.

HALA: What are you two doing up?

AHMED: She thinks she is composing. Here, in the dark.

IRENE: The lights are off so I don't disturb Mama. She has seemed upset lately. Have either of you noticed? *(She looks up for a minute at her father, challenging.)*

AHMED: No.

*(*IRENE *goes back to writing on her sheet, feigning that she is absorbed in her work but is clearly distracted)*

AHMED: Wouldn't it be better to compose in the daytime? At a piano?

IRENE: Did Beethoven, while he was deaf at the end of his life, need a piano to compose?

HALA: Aren't you taking yourself a little too seriously, Irene?

IRENE: *(Puts down her pencil)* I have to take myself seriously, Aunty. If I didn't, I couldn't get out of bed in the morning.

AHMED: If you don't go to sleep, you also can't get out of bed in the morning. So, come on, Irene. Hit the sheets.

IRENE: Can't. I've got work to do. And I'm not bothering anyone as long as I stay in the dark. Why are you up, Dad?

AHMED: I...couldn't sleep. I thought a glass of tea might help.

IRENE: Tea keeps you up, Dad.

AHMED: You're right. Okay, you two. I'll see you in the morning. Good night.

*(*AHMED *exits.* HALA *turns on the light.)*

IRENE: Leave it off. The light will bother my mom.

HALA: She's already asleep. Can I see what you're doing?

IRENE: No. I don't think it would interest you.

HALA: I do know a thing or two about music, Irene.

IRENE: Don't you think you would have gotten further if you did?

HALA: Not everybody had the opportunities you had.

IRENE: Not everyone deserves them.

HALA: You think you deserve to be safe and comfortable and well-fed more than me? More than your mother?

IRENE: You're the last person to bring up what my mother deserves.

HALA: All I want to say is that the scores I saw in your room were quite good.

IRENE: Don't look at my stuff.

HALA: Don't keep it lying around.

IRENE: It's my room.

HALA: The point is I think you should show them to your uncle Abe.

IRENE: My mom would never let me speak to him.

HALA: I bet if your mother asked him to help you, he would.

IRENE: Why don't you just go to bed, Aunty?

HALA: Do you want to talk?

IRENE: Talk about what?

HALA: So, you don't want to talk. Irene, people make mistakes and, in your lifetime, you will make your share.

IRENE: Not me. Not some mistakes. Don't act like mistakes are accidents. They're not. They're choices people make without caring that there will be consequences.

HALA: Sometimes you know there will be consequences but you don't understand the full extent of them at the time. You miscalculate the cost of your choices. I made a mistake and it will never happen again.

IRENE: Whatever. You know, speaking of calculating costs, Aunty—

HALA: Yes?

IRENE: Well, I'm kind of embarrassed to bring this up, my mother is really soft-hearted and doesn't want to turn you out or anything, but we are having a hard time making ends meet—

HALA: I see.

IRENE: And, since my dad was a fairly well-known musician in his day, it seems to make sense that he should be the one to teach me Arabic music.

HALA: That does make sense.

IRENE: I'm glad you think so. So, has Uncle Abe offered to get you an apartment yet?

HALA: No.

IRENE: What a shame. He obviously doesn't find you as charming as we do.

HALA: Are you really trying to get me to go, kid? Think about it. Think about it really good.

IRENE: Of course it's not what I want. I'm just thinking of your best interests.

HALA: If I leave here, I have to go back to Jordan. That's the only country that will give me citizenship.

IRENE: I hear it's nice there.

HALA: Not from your mother. Or from me. Do you know why we hate it? Do you know what happened to us there?

IRENE: You know that I don't.

HALA: You come from a long line of people with delusions of grandeur. In other words, idiots. The biggest one of all was your grandfather. He thought he was a leader. My mother and your mother—and all of the people in our camp—adored him. But I could see through all that—he was a joke and I was the kid of someone who cared for lost causes and other people's children more than he cared for his own. I hated his guts for it. He should have known you don't flee the Israelis to Jordan, then try to fight the Israelis when they're both working together. To be fair, the poor bastard didn't know that Hussein—I won't call him king, I won't call any man king—would sent his soldiers to clean up the camps of revolutionaries. Scores had to be settled. We were living through a Black September but we didn't know it—we thought we were just having breakfast—and in they came and I see them hit and hit and hit my dad and my mom is crawling, then the man with the cigar says "get the little one" and the biggest one comes towards me. Karema is half-asleep—

IRENE: What? What did they do to my mother?

HALA: Nothing. They left her alone.

IRENE: Why would they do that? Why would they hurt everyone and leave her alone?

HALA: I don't know.

IRENE: Why are you telling me this, Aunty?

HALA: Because what happened to your mother and her sister affects you in a thousand ways that you yourself will never be able to explain.

IRENE: Am I supposed to feel sorry for you now, Aunty?

HALA: Kind of. But, I also thought you should know your own history. I thought you would want to.

IRENE: Too bad I don't know how much of what you told me is actually true.

HALA: Ask your mother.

IRENE: There are many things I'm not going to bother my mother with unless I *have* to. Regardless, I'm glad you agree that it's best that you go.

*(*HALA *exits into* IRENE*'s bedroom, leaving* IRENE *alone on-stage.)*

Scene Eight

(The next morning. KAREMA *walks in and out of the door to the kitchen, wearing a robe and carrying small dishes of Middle Eastern food. She stops by* IRENE*'s door, hesitates, and then knocks softly.)*

KAREMA: Irene.

*(*HALA *exits from the bathroom, fully dressed.)*

HALA: She's still in bed.

KAREMA: She never sleeps in. *(Calling)* Irene, come help me set the table. *(Begins setting it herself)*

HALA: She was up late last night composing. I'll set it. It's the least I can do. Actually, it's the most—you know how useless I am in the kitchen.

*(*HALA *and* KAREMA *set the table.* AHMED *saunters in, looking tired.* KAREMA *leaves* HALA *setting the table and goes to him.)*

KAREMA: Ahmed, I have something to confess. Please don't be angry.

AHMED: What?

KAREMA: Don't be mad, okay? I thought it would be good to offer to pay Goldman to help Irene and they hung up on me—

AHMED: Oh.

KAREMA: You're not angry?

AHMED: No.

KAREMA: What are we going to tell Irene?

AHMED: Just don't tell her. She'll figure out sooner or later that no answer is an answer.

(The tea kettle whistles.)

KAREMA: I hate that sound.

*(*KAREMA *goes back into the kitchen. The whistling stops.)*

*(*AHMED *and* HALA *are alone.)*

*(*KAREMA *reenters with a steaming tea kettle.* KAREMA *goes to* IRENE*'s door.)*

KAREMA: Irene, your aunt has already set the table. Please join us. We miss you, *habibtey*. Get up, sunshine!

*(*IRENE *[Also in pajamas] enters from her bedroom, looking tired.)*

IRENE: I'm not hungry.

KAREMA: Well, come and sit with us.

IRENE: Why?

KAREMA: Irene, this is our only day off and I don't get to see you.

IRENE: Okay, okay! *(She sits down.)*

HALA: Good morning.

IRENE: You're up early. And dressed too.

HALA: It happens.

*(*KAREMA *pours tea for everyone and they pass plates around.* AHMED *and* KAREMA *eat.* HALA *puts food in her plate but does not eat.* IRENE *sits morosely.)*

HALA: This is the first time we've all sat down together, isn't it?

*(*AHMED *nods.)*

KAREMA: *(Not paying attention to* HALA*)* Irene, eat just a little of the eggs. Dad made it the way you like it. No paprika.

IRENE: No thanks.

*(*KAREMA *puts a big chunk of omelet in* IRENE*'s plate.)*

IRENE: Don't do that.

KAREMA: You have to have something.

IRENE: What do you hear out of? I said I'm not hungry.

AHMED: Let the kid do what she wants, Karema.

KAREMA: She has to have something.

HALA: I'm going to be leaving soon.

*(*AHMED *looks stunned.)*

KAREMA: What?

HALA: *(Looking at* IRENE*)* I'm going to go back to Jordan. Tonight, actually.

KAREMA: Why, Hala? You'd never choose to go back there.

IRENE: Maybe she likes Jordan, Mom.

KAREMA: No one likes Jordan. It's a place you end up, not a place you go. Where will you live, Hala? With what money?

AHMED: Uh...um...I can go with her. Help her get settled.

(Pause. IRENE *fixates her eyes on her father and begins to stare his down.* AHMED *doesn't meet her gaze.)*

KAREMA: *(Looking confused for a moment)* Oh, Ahmed. Always looking for an excuse to go to Jordan. No one is going, including you, Hala. You'll stay here. At least till your visa runs out.

IRENE: Hello! I think it's Aunty's decision, Mom.

KAREMA: Have I not been a good host to you, Sister?

HALA: No, it's not that.

AHMED: *(Speaking pleadingly to* HALA*)* We're going to move into one of our apartments soon. We'll have more space. You can have your own room, Hala.

KAREMA: What are you talking about? We're not moving and she's not leaving. *(To* HALA*)* Irene doesn't mind sharing a room with you.

HALA: Thank you for your hospitality. But, I'm leaving tomorrow.

KAREMA: No, you're not. If you're going, you'll go in a few weeks when Irene is off school. I've been wanting to take Irene to Palestine and we'll stop by Jordan first—

IRENE: Hell no.

AHMED: I want to go to Jordan!

KAREMA: Ahmed...

AHMED: We can all go. Let's all go.

KAREMA: What about the store? You went last time. It's me and Irene's turn.

IRENE: I can't leave and neither can you, Dad! Goldman is going to call any minute.

AHMED: It's probably a scam, Irene.

IRENE: A scam? What kind of scam?

AHMED: I bet he is one of those guys that you hear about that charges singers a fortune to make a demo tape.

HALA: Oh, Ahmed. If it was a scam, he would have called.

IRENE: That's right. He would have called, Dad. Not once, but ten times.

KAREMA: *(Looking at* IRENE *who is staring her father down).* Can we not discuss this now? Let's just eat our food.

AHMED: He's not the only producer in the world. I think it's important to be honest with ourselves, Irene, and acknowledge that maybe he just isn't interested.

IRENE: I think it's also important to be honest with others, Dad, and acknowledge when they are *(Gets up and picks up a handful of the omelet in her plate and flings it at* AHMED*)* dirty piece of shit assholes.

KAREMA: Irene!

AHMED: *(Stands up)* That's it. Pick up this mess!

IRENE: You pick it up!

AHMED: You may not like what I have to say, but you better respect me. I'm your father.

KAREMA: Sit down, both of you!

IRENE: Some father you are!

AHMED: I won't be bullied in my own house. You got something on your mind, kid? Say it. Or else you'd better start acting normal.

IRENE: You act normal!

KAREMA: I said, sit down.

IRENE: If I had a father like Abe, he could help me [get somewhere]—

AHMED: If you had talent, you could help yourself.

*(*IRENE *gets up and heads towards her bedroom.)*

KAREMA: Irene! He didn't mean it.

*(*IRENE *slams the door.)*

KAREMA: That wasn't necessary, Ahmed. Go apologize.

(The sound of a very loud and vulgar Prince song bursts out.)

AHMED: Lower that shit. *(Pause)* Lower it or I'm coming in there.

(The music is silenced.)

KAREMA: You go apologize right now.

*(*AHMED *heads towards the bedroom and slams the door.* KAREMA *sits at the table with* HALA.*)*

KAREMA: I just wanted us to have a nice meal. I don't know what's gotten in to everyone in this house.

*(*KAREMA *begins to pick up the eggs from the floor.* HALA *helps her.)*

*(*IRENE *enters from her room with a bag and her scores in her hand. She heads straight to the door.)*

KAREMA: Where are you going, Irene?

IRENE: Library.

KAREMA: Isn't it closed on Sundays?

*(*IRENE *slams the door.)*

KAREMA: I'm worried about that girl.

HALA: I'm not.

KAREMA: I'm worried about you. So, what's the grand plan? The great scheme? Come on, fill me in. Why are you leaving?

HALA: I just don't like America.

KAREMA: But you hate Jordan.

HALA: I want to really try my music again.

KAREMA: Be a teacher?

HALA: No, a singer.

KAREMA: That's just not realistic, Hala.

*(*AHMED *enters from his bedroom with his* tubleh *in hand.)*

KAREMA: Where are you going?

AHMED: To fix a toilet.

KAREMA: Which apartment?

(He slams the door on his way out. KAREMA *and* HALA *are alone again.)*

KAREMA: *(To* HALA*)* Why did you go through all that trouble to get a visa if you're not even going to give it a try? We can hire a lawyer, maybe get you asylum here.

HALA: No. I came because I thought it was going to work with Abe. But, he isn't how I remember. He used to lower his voice when he spoke to me—I don't think even he realized it. When it got bad in Kuwait, I began to think about him again—how someone once treated me like I would break...well, that's over. Look, I need to borrow your husband for a few weeks.

KAREMA: What? What do you mean "borrow my husband"?

HALA: I didn't tell you everything that happened in Jordan, but suffice it to say I don't know anyone who would rent me a room.

KAREMA: Hala, you can't ask a wife to let you borrow her husband. I can go with you.

HALA: Won't work. I need a man and I can find one quicker when I have one on my arm. He won't mind. He likes Jordan.

KAREMA: Hala!

HALA: It's not a big deal. I'm not going to do anything with him.

(Pause)

KAREMA: Um... Uh... Um. Did you sleep with my husband?

HALA: No.

KAREMA: You're lying. The only time you answer a direct question directly is when you're lying. You can't do this in my house. Not here, Hala! Not here!

HALA: For a few weeks is all I'm asking.

KAREMA: You were born fucked up and there's no excuses for it! *(She shakes* HALA.*)* I don't care what happened. Just stop this talk! Stop it! Stop it!

HALA: *(Pulls herself free)* I need him, Karema. For a few weeks. He'll help me get set up and he'll come back.

KAREMA: If he goes, I can't have him back. Husbands are not like sisters, Hala. When it breaks, it's broken!

HALA: You have everything.

KAREMA: He can't have my husband! I never thought you would stoop this low, that you were this fucked-up!

HALA: You're just as fucked up as I am. At least I don't go around pretending I'm fine.

KAREMA: He's my husband, Hala. This is my home. You're going to need my help again and I'll have to—

HALA: I won't need your damn help!

KAREMA: —give it to you, because you're my sister. Only when you're dead will I be free.

HALA: You're free all right! You left! *(Pushes her)* You abandoned me and you knew you were one person I needed.

KAREMA: *(Pushes her back)* Did you want me to stay in that place?!

HALA: We could have figured a way to get out together. But, no, you weren't waiting for me. Married the first boy you found with a visa to America just like you said you would.

KAREMA: I was scared. I was so scared it would happen again.

HALA: So you leave me there alone? With our parents who couldn't even look me in the eye? You took care of Karema first, you always take care of Karema, and that meant leaving me so you could forget—

KAREMA: I couldn't forget! I knew to keep my eyes down, Hala. You didn't.

HALA: You're blaming me?!

KAREMA: No, I'm blaming me. I was trying to tell you to keep yours eyes down, Hala, do what I'm doing. They're beating Dad, keep your eyes down. They tearing Mom's clothes, keep your eyes down. I should have told you with real words, a little pinch, but I'm afraid to call attention to myself so I keep trying to tell you from my mind to yours—copy me like you always do—don't look at people who can't look at themselves. But it's too late.

(KAREMA *exits into her room, crying.* HALA *lights a cigarette shakily.)*

Scene Nine

*(*AHMED *enters with his* tubleh *in its case in his hand.* HALA *is sitting at the table and she lights another cigarette.)*

HALA: I told Karema.

AHMED: What? What did you tell my wife?

HALA: That you want to come with me.

AHMED: I never said that. You had no right. You didn't even tell me you were going.

(KAREMA *emerges from her room. She stands in front of the door with her arms folded and looks at* AHMED.)

*(*HALA *stands up and exits into* IRENE*'s bedroom.)*

AHMED: Karema, I have to go.

(Pause. KAREMA *heads past* AHMED *and begins to clear the table frenetically.)*

AHMED: Karema. I don't know what Hala told you. This isn't about your sister for me. I don't belong here. You know that. I always planned to go back. You know that.

*(*IRENE *enters from the front door.* AHMED *turns and goes to her.* KAREMA *keeps clearing the table, hitting the dishes against each other a little too hard.)*

AHMED: Irene. I'm sorry about what I said this morning—

IRENE: Whatever, Dad.

(Pause)

IRENE: What's going on? Mom?

AHMED: You know I love you. You know I'd give my...life for you, but I can't...live my life for you. No one likes the music I can make here. You, of all people, should understand that.

IRENE: Dad? What are you saying? Are you going with her?

AHMED: Uh...I...

IRENE: No, please, Dad. She's just a lying whore.

AHMED: It's not about her.

IRENE: You were kissing her right here!

*(*KAREMA *looks at* AHMED*. Then, she grabs a pile of dishes and rushes into the kitchen.)*

AHMED: Please, Irene. You have to understand. This is between your mother and I. It has nothing to do with you.

IRENE: It should have everything to do with me,
you both should stay together because of me.
Mom, do something!

AHMED: Irene, would you stay a place where you couldn't sing?

IRENE: Oh, come on. You just want to fuck Aunty Hala.

(IRENE *runs to her room and tries the door. It's locked.)*

IRENE: She's here?! She's here. Get out of my room, you whore. Get out.

KAREMA: Stop it, Irene.

IRENE: Mom, tell him he can't go.

KAREMA: I can't stop him. *(To* AHMED*) If* you're going to leave, leave now. Take this with you. *(She goes to the door and throws out the* tubleh.*)*

AHMED: My father gave me that.

KAREMA: Fuck you and your father! Get out of this house!

*(*AHMED *gets the* tubleh *and reenters.)*

AHMED: I built this goddamn house with my sweat and tears. You aren't kicking me out of it!

KAREMA: *(Pushing him)* I said get out! Get out! Get out!

IRENE: Stop it, Mom. Please.

AHMED: I gave up my music, my life, for you and all I wanted was to be more than the fucking handyman.

KAREMA: You'll come crawling back. On your goddamn knees.

AHMED: I wouldn't come back if you were the
last woman on earth. Because you're not a woman.
I've been trying to love you as if you were one.

KAREMA: I did my duties as a wife. More than you deserved!

AHMED: Duties?! You put more passion into cleaning up the vomit off the storefront window! For eighteen goddamn years, I obeyed you, even if what you were asking me to do was to cut off my own balls. You wouldn't let me play my instrument in my own house. My own fucking house!

KAREMA: It made me homesick, Ahmed!

AHMED: What?

KAREMA: I thought you knew that. I thought you understood.

AHMED: I don't care if it killed you. You know what my music meant to me.

IRENE: Dad, please stay.

AHMED: Your mother never loved me, Irene. Did you, Karema?

KAREMA: Why are you trying to humiliate me? Do you want me to beg? Is that what this is about?

IRENE: Be nicer to him, Mom.

KAREMA: *(Speaking to* IRENE *and not looking at* AHMED*)* I showed him in every way possible that he was the thing that I depended on.

AHMED: What ways?

IRENE: Talk to him like he's here, Mom.

KAREMA: He's already gone.

AHMED: What ways, Karema?

KAREMA: *(Finally looking at him)* In every way I knew how.

AHMED: It wasn't enough. It wasn't even fucking close!

*(*IRENE *screams at the top of her lungs.* HALA *emerges with her luggage and her* 'oud. AHMED *goes to* IRENE.*)*

AHMED: Irene, I'm going to call every day.

IRENE: Whatever, Dad. *(To* HALA*)* and you, Aunty, I hope you....

HALA: You can't wish anything upon me that hasn't already been done. I'm leaving you my *'oud*. A prince gave it to me.

IRENE: Stop lying! Just stop lying!

HALA: Okay, I stole it. But someone *should* have given it to me.

IRENE: I'll smash it.

HALA: You're too smart to do that. My head—you might smash—but not a perfectly good instrument.

*(*HALA *goes over to* KAREMA.*)*

KAREMA: This isn't good-bye for us.

HALA: It might be.

KAREMA: You'll come back broke and need my help. This isn't good-bye.

*(*HALA *hugs* KAREMA. *After a beat,* KAREMA *grips her arms around* HALA *tightly.* HALA *disentangles from* KAREMA *and pulls away.)*

*(*AHMED *and* HALA *leave. As the door shuts behind them,* IRENE *runs to try to go after them, but* KAREMA *blocks her. Then,* KAREMA *sit and cries.)*

IRENE: What are we going to do now, Mom?

*(*KAREMA *keeps crying and does not respond.)*

IRENE: At least now I don't have to worry about whether my father is going to run off with my aunt, because my father has run off with my aunt.

(KAREMA *keeps crying.)*

IRENE: You know what? It's time to close the store for the night. We should let the workers go home.

(KAREMA *shakes her head.)*

IRENE: Please, Mom. Stop crying. Get up. You have to. For me.

KAREMA: You're not enough, Irene.

IRENE: Neither are you, but we're all we've got. Get up, Mom. I'll go with you. Please, Mom.

KAREMA: I'm afraid.

IRENE: I'm afraid too, Mom. But, we have to let the workers go home.

KAREMA: Your Goldman isn't going to ever call you, Irene.

IRENE: I know. What's that Arabic saying you and Dad always say? No answers are the answer. Or is it? Every answer is the answer. *(Pause)* Hello? I'm saying it wrong so you would correct me, Mother.

KAREMA: You should know the saying by now, Irene.

IRENE: True. Come on, let's go.

KAREMA: I can't go down there. I can't, Irene.

IRENE: Fine. I'll do it for you.

(IRENE *exits and leaves* KAREMA *alone on-stage.)*

Scene Ten

(During the transition, the tea kettle whistles. IRENE *enters from her bedroom and goes over to knock on her parents' bedroom door. She stops herself, touches the door softly, and then goes to the kitchen and turns off the kettle. Irene slips on*

a smock over her clothes [Which KAREMA *wears in earlier scenes] and exits through the front door.)*

(When IRENE *is gone,* KAREMA *enters from her bedroom and curls up on the couch.)*

ABE: *(Off-stage)* Hello?

KAREMA: *(Jumping up)* Ahmed! *(She opens the door)*

ABE: No, but close.

KAREMA: Abe, what are you doing here?

ABE: *(Puts his foot in the door)* I've been officially invited. Your daughter asked me to come. What for? I don't know. She said she needed a favor and wanted to ask in person.

KAREMA: Irene's in the store, Abe. The entrance is right downstairs.

ABE: Well, she asked me to meet her here. *(Pause)* You're not going to make me wait outside, are you?

*(*KAREMA *steps aside and* ABE *enters.* ABE *sits down.* KAREMA *remains standing.)*

ABE: What is that wonderful smell? Fresh falafel! God, how I would like some fresh falafel if only someone would be kind enough to offer it to me.

(Long pause)

KAREMA: Would you like some?

ABE: Can't. I'm a diet, but thanks for so kindly offering. *(Putting his feet up on the coffee table.)* It's been a while since you actually let me through the front door of your home, Karema. How long has it been?

KAREMA: A while.

ABE: It's been ten years since you cursed me terribly, and threw me out of your home without letting me finish my dinner. Ten years. Time flies. Does it not, Karema?

(Pause)

KAREMA: Abe, I don't know why my daughter would invite you here.

ABE: She's probably going to ask again for me to do something to support her singing career that my company can't afford. But I figured I'd hear the kid out. Where is Hala?

KAREMA: She isn't here.

ABE: And Ahmed?

KAREMA: He's not *(Pause)* home.

ABE: So, here we are. All alone. You and I.

KAREMA: I'll call Irene—

ABE: Don't bother. I can wait. Hala hasn't dropped by or called in a few weeks. Any idea why?

KAREMA: Perhaps she's upset that you won't marry her.

ABE: *(Getting ruffled for the first time)* She knows I can't do that.

KAREMA: *(With just a hint of sarcasm)* She doesn't exactly fit into your new lifestyle now, does she?

ABE: Don't start.

KAREMA: Okay.

ABE: Well, that was easy. You know me better than that. I don't enjoy hollow victories. Come on. Let's see you shriek about how by aping another race, I'm admitting that I think I am no better than an ape.

KAREMA: You aren't.

ABE: I know. So, come on, tell me how I will die surrounded by strangers, cursing myself in my mother tongue. That—in particular—I was looking forward to the entire ride over here.

KAREMA: I'm not all that bad.

ABE: You're worse. Come on. Give it to me.

KAREMA: What do you want me to say?

ABE: What you always say.

KAREMA: What for, Abe?

ABE: So I can respond the way I always respond, which is it costs me more than it ever gave me to deny who I am. I'm sorry that I lied about my background when I was young and scared and had just been abandoned by a woman I intended to marry for a man with a little more money—

KAREMA: A lot more.

ABE: Okay. A lot more. Though I soon changed that. It's not like I converted or anything. I know it was stupid to lie. I thought it was the only way I could make it here. I never told you the story about how I started pretending to be a Jew. Aren't you even a little curious? Why won't you ever hear me out?

KAREMA: Okay.

ABE: What did you just say? Okay?! This is so unexpected, I almost don't know how to respond. Good thing that over the years I've given a thought or two to what I'd say if I had the chance to actually talk to you. *(Pause.)* Now, picture this. You walk into a job interview, someone mispronounces your name, makes a false assumption. You don't correct them—

KAREMA:
I would correct them!

ABE: *(At the same time)*
You get the job,

ABE: *(Ignoring* KAREMA*'s outburst and continuing without a break)* it becomes too late to correct them.

KAREMA: It's a deliberate [lie]—

ABE: It wasn't deliberate, Karema. I mean, it didn't start out that way. The guy who interviewed me, Ben, was a nice guy. He died recently. You would have liked him, Karema.

KAREMA: I don't think so.

ABE: I do. It was my first interview to be an assistant in the music industry. He asked me where I came from and I told him Egypt.

KAREMA: First lie right there.

ABE: But it wasn't really. I had lived in Egypt for six months before coming to the States. Egypt had just made peace with Israel. And I thought if I flat out told him I was a Palestinian, I'd never get the job. Then, he said, "there were lots of Jews in Egypt before all the troubles" and I said "yes, there were a lot of Jews living in Egypt." So what if I somehow failed to mention that I wasn't one of them?

KAREMA: What do you mean "so what"?

ABE: I don't lie anymore. I keep to myself and I don't answer questions about my personal life. That's what I say now when people ask me anything. I don't answer questions. Do you know how much money I give to our people?

KAREMA: It won't correct it.

ABE: And how much of your income do you donate?

KAREMA: I...uh...

ABE: Zilch. That's what I thought. Where is Irene? I'm sick of you already. I can't believe I was a coin toss away from being your husband. Imagine! If I had married you, I would have to spend every night fighting with you like this.

(Pause)

KAREMA: *(Furious)* Married me?! Have you gone crazy?

ABE: Ah, there's the Karema that I've been missing. You would have fallen for me. I couldn't play music and make fancy speeches like Ahmed could, but you would have fallen hard just the same. But I lost the coin toss—

KAREMA: You'd better explain before I toss a coin [down your throat]—

ABE: And every time I see the fury in your face I thank God for the force of gravity and motion He put in place that made that coin in that corner of our universe face the way it did that day. You really don't know what I'm talking about, do you?

KAREMA: No idea. Why don't you meet my daughter downstairs? *(Walks towards the door and opens in an inch)*

ABE: *(Walks to the door, perhaps a little nearer than he needs to be to* KAREMA *and shuts the door)* So Ahmed never told you? After all these years! You see, he and I liked you and Hala. We used to call you two the Hurricane and the Quiet Storm. We both couldn't decide which sister liked better.

KAREMA: Well, I know I never would have—

ABE: Let me finish my story. We agreed to flip a coin and stay away from the woman the winner chose. We saw that in an American movie somewhere, flipping a coin for a woman. Ahmed picked heads, I picked tails. Ahmed flipped and, because God is great, it was heads.

KAREMA: I never would have stomached you for a minute. You are part of our race like vomit is part of a human body. It's a relief to be rid of you.

ABE: I lost. Thank God. Because if I had won, there's a possibility I might have chosen you.

IRENE: *(Entering and dressed in* KAREMA*'s smock)* Hi, Uncle. I'm so sorry to keep you waiting.

ABE: No problem. I was just having a friendly little chat with your mom. Isn't it a bit late to be working?

IRENE: I had to wait for our last delivery.

KAREMA: Why did you invite him here?

IRENE: Have you told him about Aunty Hala and Dad?

KAREMA: It's none of his business.

ABE: What about Hala and Ahmed?

IRENE: A few weeks ago, my father and Aunty Hala ran off together.

ABE: What do you mean "ran off"?

KAREMA: What do you think it means?

IRENE: Mom, just be quiet. We know they've gone to Jordan together. *(Getting choked up)* They haven't contacted us yet. It feels like they never will.

ABE: Oh, my God. That woman...left me again...with my pain in the ass brother! And for Ahmed to leave you two...alone...

IRENE: We don't know what to do. I have been staying home from school since they left because my mom... well, she hasn't been able to work. I know this isn't your problem. I wouldn't turn to you if I didn't have to. You know that I wanted to be a singer.

ABE: I know. And, like I said, when you visited me with your father, college is much more practical.

IRENE: I realize that. Singing is such a long shot. But I want to do the next best thing—which is to go into the music business and help other artists realize their dreams. So would it be possible for me to work for you? As an assistant, perhaps?

KAREMA: Over my dead body.

IRENE: If that's what it takes.

ABE: Irene!

IRENE: *(To* ABE*)* Don't worry, Uncle. My mother and I just like to tease one another. I will take the G E D test and go to college at night. That's the only way I can feasibly go at all. Then, we can close the store and I can take care of my mother. Of course, I will be discreet about our relationship. I was planning on changing my last name anyway to something easier to pronounce.

ABE: No! Don't do that. It's not necessary. If you make people money, trust me, they learn to pronounce your name. Don't try to mask who you are, because, if you do, nothing you achieve will be worth a damn. Also, it's extremely stressful. Do you know how much Yiddish I had to pretend to understand over the years?

IRENE: Okay, I just didn't want people thinking I got a job because I'm your niece.

ABE: Irene, I have a very small office and I'm really [not able to]—

KAREMA: We need help. We need *your* help

(Pause)

ABE: Well, there might be something I can do. But, as you know so well, Karema, nothing in this life is free. I miss Arabic food. Invite me over for dinner every Sunday, and I can probably get Irene a job.

KAREMA: What?

IRENE: You're welcome to eat here every day, Uncle. Our house is your house.

KAREMA: I'll poison you.

IRENE: I'll taste the food beforehand to make sure she doesn't.

ABE: I'll hold you to that promise, kid. What do you say, Karema? I'm giving your daughter a full-time job, entry-level, of course.

IRENE: Of course.

ABE: In exchange, you give me a simple meal once a week. Maybe when I taste how good your food is, it'll give me strength. To do the things I should do.

(Pause)

IRENE: Come on, Mom.

KAREMA: All right, all right. Since you give me no choice.

ABE: Fabulous. Irene, get to my office tomorrow by eight.

IRENE: Eight?! That's earlier than school!

ABE: Is there a problem with that?

IRENE: No. Not at all.

ABE: Good. I won't be there. My assistant will tell you what to do.

IRENE: I'm very grateful.

ABE: *(Looking at* KAREMA*)* Is everyone here grateful?

*(*KAREMA *glares at him.)*

ABE: I take it that means yes. Until Sunday. *(He steps towards the door, but turns around to grab a falafel that is on a plate on the table.)*

*(*ABE *takes a bite then exits.* IRENE *runs to the window to watch him go and the sound of a car pulling away can be heard.)*

IRENE: *(Doing a little victory dance)* He's giving me a job! He actually bought that whole I-want-to-help-other-artists bullshit.

KAREMA: I told you he wasn't very bright.

IRENE: Or maybe he's just a nice man and wanted to give me a job.

KAREMA: Nice men don't lie about who they are.

IRENE: Oh, Mom. Nice men do a lot worse than that. Thanks for letting him in.

KAREMA: I said I would. But, Abe came early and I *(Pause)* thought it was your father.

(Pause)

IRENE: Oh. *(Pause)* I miss Dad, Mom. Do you think he'll call us again?

KAREMA: I know he will. He's burning through his credit cards.

IRENE: So?

KAREMA: So that means Hala won't stay with him long.

IRENE: Even if she leaves him, he'll stay in Jordan. He loves it there.

KAREMA: Don't worry about your father. You'll always have me hanging around your neck like a dead weight. That you can count on.

IRENE: You know it seems Uncle Abe had a crush on you. We've spent all week planning what I should say to him and it turns out all along that all you had to do was bat your big brown eyes.

KAREMA: You're not too old to be hit, Irene.

IRENE: And apparently you're not too old to be hit on, Mom. I overheard what he said.

KAREMA: How dare you eavesdrop!

IRENE: It's a small house, Mom. You can't help but hear what goes on in it whether or not you want to.

KAREMA: Well, to hear what was going on from outside, it's pretty clear that you had to want to. You should appreciate that I'm doing all this for you. You should be grateful. He's forcing me to—

IRENE: Yeah, right. I believe that.

KAREMA: If I'm being civil to Abe, I'm doing it for you and for our people. I'm going to convince him that he cannot go on pretending to be a Jew.

IRENE: I have a feeling you can convince Uncle Abe of anything.

KAREMA: You're probably getting all the price tags mixed up. I should go downstairs.

IRENE: No. I meant what I said about us closing the store.

KAREMA: We can't afford—

IRENE: How many apartments do we have, Mom?

KAREMA: Not so many and they're in a run down neighborhood.

IRENE: Bloomfield Hills in the richest district in the entire Detroit area.

KAREMA: That isn't saying much.

IRENE: I want to know how many we have. I can find out without you. All I have to do is [call up]—

KAREMA: Twenty.

IRENE: Twenty?! We are collecting rent on twenty apartments! Well, it's going to be nineteen. Because we are kicking someone out and moving into one of them tomorrow.

KAREMA: We can't afford to—

IRENE: Yes, we can. I've got a job now too. It'll be boring, dull, repetitive, but maybe my uncle will let me use the recording studio after hours. Then, maybe he'll listen to my songs and maybe he'll like them. Because maybe—out of the millions of songs I'll make—there will be one or two that is the kind of song that, when you hear the first note, you know you have to stick around to hear the last. Do you think it will work, Mom? Do you think I can make it work?

KAREMA: Maybe.

END OF PLAY

CPSIA information can be obtained
at www.ICGtesting.com
Printed in the USA
LVHW011706160719
624282LV00016B/1117/P